The Very Best of Ralph Waldo Emerson

DAVID GRAHAM

ISBN: 150243718X
ISBN-13: 978-1502437181

DISCLAIMER

Although every effort has been taken to ensure all
information in this book is accurate, human error is always
a possibility and therefore the author apologises in the
event of any inaccuracies.

CONTENTS

INTRODUCTION

Ralph Waldo Emerson was without doubt one of the greatest minds of the 19th century. Known mainly for his poetry, literature and lecturing, he was also a great philosopher and much of what he said holds as true now as it did 200 years ago.

Emerson talked extensively of nature, as well as God. However, his true religious beliefs are debatable and he is considered by many as a pantheist; that is to say he believed God was part of the universe itself rather than a separate entity.

Many of his philosophies were striking and he has remained a much quoted figure to this day.

This book brings together some of his most fascinating thoughts on a variety of subjects.

PHILOSOPHY

"We must be our own before we can be another's."

*

"Science does not know its debt to imagination."

*

"Common sense is genius dressed in its working clothes."

*

"There is always safety in valor."

*

"Win as if you were used to it, lose as if you enjoyed it for a change."

*

"There is a tendency for things to right themselves."

*

"We acquire the strength we have overcome."

*

"No change of circumstances can repair a defect of character."

*

"Death comes to all, but great achievements build a monument which shall endure until the sun grows cold."

*

"Unless you try to do something beyond what you have already mastered, you will never grow."

*

"Nothing external to you has any power over you."

*

"The years teach much which the days never know."

*

"We find delight in the beauty and happiness of children that makes the heart too big for the body."

*

"The greatest gift is a portion of thyself."

*

"Wisdom has its root in goodness, not goodness its root in wisdom."

*

"If you would lift me up you must be on higher ground."

*

"Use what language you will, you can never say anything but what you are."

*

"The invariable mark of wisdom is to see the miraculous in the common."

*

"Write it on your heart that every day is the best day in the year."

*

"The sky is the daily bread of the eyes."

*

"Beauty without expression is boring."

*

"Truth is beautiful, without doubt; but so are lies."

*

"Who hears me, who understands me, becomes mine, a possession for all time."

*

"The end of the human race will be that it will eventually die of civilization."

*

"Nobody can bring you peace but yourself."

*

"Knowledge is knowing that we cannot know."

*

"Let us be silent, that we may hear the whispers of the gods."

*

"Every man I meet is in some way my superior."

*

"Our faith comes in moments; our vice is habitual."

*

"Happy is the hearing man; unhappy the speaking man."

*

"We are rich only through what we give, and poor only through what we refuse."

*

"What we seek we shall find; what we flee from flees from us."

*

"A great part of courage is the courage of having done the thing before."

*

"Can anything be so elegant as to have few wants, and to serve them one's self?"

*

"Reality is a sliding door."

*

"Do not go where the path may lead, go instead
where there is no path and leave a trail."

*

"A man is relieved and gay when he has put his heart
into his work and done his best; but what he has said
or done otherwise shall give him no peace."

*

"A man is what he thinks about all day long."

*

"Beauty without grace is the hook without the bait."

*

"This time, like all times, is a very good one, if we but know what to do with it."

*

"Make the most of yourself, for that is all there is of you."

*

"Every wall is a door."

*

"What lies behind you and what lies in front of you, pales in comparison to what lies inside of you."

*

"Who you are speaks so loudly I can't hear what you're saying."

*

"Fiction reveals truth that reality obscures."

*

"Power and speed be hands and feet."

*

"Give a boy address and accomplishments and you give him the mastery of palaces and fortunes where he goes."

*

"There are as many pillows of illusion as flakes in a snow-storm. We wake from one dream into another dream."

*

"Truth is the property of no individual but is the treasure of all men."

*

"Enthusiasm is the mother of effort, and without it nothing great was ever achieved."

*

"The value of a principle is the number of things it will explain."

*

"The ancestor of every action is a thought."

*

"The faith that stands on authority is not faith."

*

"Great geniuses have the shortest biographies."

*

"It is the quality of the moment, not the number of

days, or events, or of actors, that imports."

*

"It was high counsel that I once heard given to a young person, 'always do what you are afraid to do.'"

*

"The real and lasting victories are those of peace, and not of war."

*

"A hero is no braver than an ordinary man, but he is brave five minutes longer."

*

"Don't be too timid and squeamish about your actions. All life is an experiment."

*

"Little minds have little worries, big minds have no time for worries."

＊

"Always do what you are afraid to do."

＊

"Genius always finds itself a century too early."

＊

"The desire of gold is not for gold. It is for the means of freedom and benefit."

＊

"Fate is nothing but the deeds committed in a prior state of existence."

＊

"If the stars should appear but one night every

thousand years how man would marvel and stare."

*

"Life consists in what a man is thinking of all day."

*

"An ounce of action is worth a ton of theory."

*

"We are always getting ready to live but never living."

*

"The secret of ugliness consists not in irregularity, but in being uninteresting."

*

"As we grow old, the beauty steals inward."

*

"Curiosity is lying in wait for every secret."

*

"Each age, it is found, must write its own books; or rather, each generation for the next succeeding."

*

"Every spirit makes its house, and we can give a shrewd guess from the house to the inhabitant."

*

"Our best thoughts come from others."

*

"A man in debt is so far a slave."

*

EMERSON

ect are two sides of one fact."

*

"In skating over thin ice our safety is in our speed."

*

"Trust your instinct to the end, though you can render no reason."

*

"Though we travel the world over to find the beautiful, we must carry it with us or we find it not."

*

"Passion rebuilds the world for the youth. It makes all things alive and significant."

*

"Nothing great was ever achieved without
enthusiasm."

*

"For every minute you remain angry, you give up sixty
seconds of peace of mind."

*

"There is an optical illusion about every person we
meet."

*

"Every man in his lifetime needs to thank his faults."

*

"We gain the strength of the temptation we resist."

*

"Our greatest glory is not in never failing, but in rising

up every time we fail."

*

"Build a better mousetrap and the world will beat a
path to your door."

*

"Great hearts steadily send forth the secret forces that
incessantly draw great events."

*

"What you are comes to you."

*

"Do the thing we fear, and death of fear is certain."

*

"People seem not to see that their opinion of the
world is also a confession of character."

*

"Once you make a decision, the universe conspires to make it happen."

*

"With the past, I have nothing to do; nor with the future. I live now."

*

"He who is not everyday conquering some fear has not learned the secret of life."

*

"No man ever prayed heartily without learning something."

*

"Every mind must make its choice between truth and

repose. It cannot have both."

*

"The world is all gates, all opportunities, strings of tension waiting to be struck."

*

"Before we acquire great power we must acquire wisdom to use it well."

*

"Every experiment, by multitudes or by individuals, that has a sensual and selfish aim, will fail."

*

"Children are all foreigners."

*

"To be yourself in a world that is constantly trying to

make you something else is the greatest
accomplishment."

*

"To be great is to be misunderstood."

*

"Truth is handsomer than the affectation of love.
Your goodness must have some edge to it, else it is
none."

*

"It is one of the beautiful compensations in this life
that no one can sincerely try to help another without
helping himself."

*

"The first wealth is health."

*

"Every fact is related on one side to sensation, and, on the other, to morals. The game of thought is, on the appearance of one of these two sides, to find the other: given the upper, to find the under side."

*

"Make yourself necessary to somebody."

*

"Trust men and they will be true to you; treat them greatly and they will show themselves great."

*

"The revelation of thought takes men out of servitude into freedom."

*

"For everything you have missed, you have gained something else, and for everything you gain, you lose something else."

*

"The sum of wisdom is that time is never lost that is
devoted to work."

*

"A good indignation brings out all one's powers."

*

"Mysticism is the mistake of an accidental and
individual symbol for an universal one."

ABOUT GOD

"All I have seen teaches me to trust the creator for all I have not seen."

*

"The highest revelation is that God is in every man."

*

"There is no chance and anarchy in the universe. All is system and gradation. Every god is there sitting in his sphere."

*

"God enters by a private door into every individual."

*

"We see God face to face every hour, and know the savor of Nature."

*

"Never lose an opportunity of seeing anything beautiful, for beauty is God's handwriting."

ABOUT MANKIND

"As long as a man stands in his own way, everything seems to be in his way."

*

"We are born believing. A man bears beliefs as a tree bears apples."

*

"A foolish consistency is the hobgoblin of little minds, adored by little statesmen and philosophers and divines."

*

"The man of genius inspires us with a boundless confidence in our own powers."

*

"We are a puny and fickle folk. Avarice, hesitation, and following are our diseases."

*

"Men love to wonder, and that is the seed of science."

*

"No great man ever complains of want of opportunity."

*

"People that seem so glorious are all show; underneath they are like everyone else."

*

"The civilized man has built a coach, but has lost the use of his feet."

*

"Every man is a quotation from all his ancestors."

*

"A great man is always willing to be little."

*

"Men's actions are too strong for them. Show me a man who has acted, and who has not been the victim and slave of his action."

*

"All mankind love a lover."

*

"In the morning a man walks with his whole body; in the evening, only with his legs."

*

"Men admire the man who can organize their wishes and thoughts in stone and wood and steel and brass."

*

"Our chief want is someone who will inspire us to be what we know we could be."

*

"We are symbols, and inhabit symbols."

*

"A man is a method, a progressive arrangement; a selecting principle, gathering his like to him; wherever he goes."

*

"There are other measures of self-respect for a man, than the number of clean shirts he puts on every day."

*

"The health of the eye seems to demand a horizon. We are never tired, so long as we can see far enough."

*

"Every man is a consumer, and ought to be a producer. He is by constitution expensive, and needs to be rich."

*

"Men are what their mothers made them."

*

"Great men or men of great gifts you shall easily find, but symmetrical men never."

*

"Great men are they who see that spiritual is stronger
than any material force - that thoughts rule the
world."

*

"Every man has his own courage, and is betrayed
because he seeks in himself the courage of other
persons."

*

"People do not seem to realize that their opinion of
the world is also a confession of character."

*

"We are by nature observers, and thereby learners.
That is our permanent state."

*

"Shallow men believe in luck. Strong men believe in cause and effect."

*

"A man is a god in ruins. When men are innocent, life shall be longer, and shall pass into the immortal, as gently as we awake from dreams."

*

"The search after the great men is the dream of youth, and the most serious occupation of manhood."

ABOUT NATURE

"What is a weed? A plant whose virtues have never been discovered."

*

"Adopt the pace of nature: her secret is patience."

*

"When nature has work to be done, she creates a genius to do it."

*

"I have no hostility to nature, but a child's love to it. I expand and live in the warm day like corn and melons."

*

"The creation of a thousand forests is in one acorn."

*

"As soon as there is life there is danger."

*

"The earth laughs in flowers."

*

"Everything in Nature contains all the powers of Nature. Everything is made of one hidden stuff."

*

"Nature is a mutable cloud which is always and never the same."

*

"Nature always wears the colors of the spirit."

*

"Flowers... are a proud assertion that a ray of beauty outvalues all the utilities of the world."

*

"Nature and books belong to the eyes that see them."

*

"Every natural fact is a symbol of some spiritual fact."

*

"Our admiration of the antique is not admiration of the old, but of the natural."

*

"The fox has many tricks. The hedgehog has but one.
But that is the best of all."

*

"Every particular in nature, a leaf, a drop, a crystal, a
moment of time is related to the whole, and partakes
of the perfection of the whole."

GENERAL THOUGHTS AND OPINIONS

"The wave of evil washes all our institutions alike."

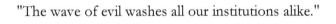

"Every artist was first an amateur."

*

"America is another name for opportunity."

*

"The martyr cannot be dishonored. Every lash inflicted is a tongue of fame; every prison a more illustrious abode."

*

"For every benefit you receive a tax is levied."

*

"There is a blessed necessity by which the interest of men is always driving them to the right; and, again, making all crime mean and ugly."

*

"The reason why the world lacks unity, and lies broken and in heaps, is, because man is disunited with himself."

*

"Fine manners need the support of fine manners in others."

*

"A chief event of life is the day in which we have encountered a mind that startled us."

*

"All life is an experiment. The more experiments you make the better."

*

"I have thought a sufficient measure of civilization is the influence of good women."

*

"Character is higher than intellect. A great soul will be strong to live as well as think."

*

"Every known fact in natural science was divined by the presentiment of somebody, before it was actually verified."

*

"Some books leave us free and some books make us free."

*

"There is creative reading as well as creative writing."

*

"As a cure for worrying, work is better than whiskey."

*

"Every actual State is corrupt. Good men must not obey laws too well."

*

"It is not length of life, but depth of life."

*

"People disparage knowing and the intellectual life, and urge doing. I am content with knowing, if only I could know."

*

"Doing well is the result of doing good. That's what capitalism is all about."

*

"When we quarrel, how we wish we had been blameless."

*

"O Day of days when we can read! The reader and the book, either without the other is naught."

*

"The reward of a thing well done is having done it."

*

"One must be an inventor to read well. There is then creative reading as well as creative writing."

*

"All diseases run into one, old age."

*

"Nothing astonishes men so much as common sense and plain dealing."

*

"I like the silent church before the service begins, better than any preaching."

*

"Hitch your wagon to a star."

*

"If the tongue had not been framed for articulation, man would still be a beast in the forest."

*

"It is said that the world is in a state of bankruptcy, that the world owes the world more than the world can pay."

*

"Pictures must not be too picturesque."

*

"You cannot do a kindness too soon, for you never know how soon it will be too late."

*

"Bad times have a scientific value. These are occasions a good learner would not miss."

*

"Fear defeats more people than any other one thing in the world."

*

"Why need I volumes, if one word suffice?"

*

"Judge of your natural character by what you do in your dreams."

*

"Society is always taken by surprise at any new example of common sense."

*

"Love of beauty is taste. The creation of beauty is art."

*

"Getting old is a fascination thing. The older you get,
the older you want to get."

*

"Every book is a quotation; and every house is a
quotation out of all forests, and mines, and stone
quarries; and every man is a quotation from all his
ancestors."

*

"We aim above the mark to hit the mark."

*

"There was never a child so lovely but his mother was
glad to get him to sleep."

*

"The age of a woman doesn't mean a thing. The best

tunes are played on the oldest fiddles."

*

"I hate quotations. Tell me what you know."

*

"Every man supposes himself not to be fully
understood or appreciated."

*

"People only see what they are prepared to see."

*

"The best effort of a fine person is felt after we have
left their presence."

*

"It is my desire, in the office of a Christian minister,
to do nothing which I cannot do with my whole

heart. Having said this, I have said all."

*

"Manners require time, and nothing is more vulgar
than haste."

*

"Money often costs too much."

*

"In art, the hand can never execute anything higher
than the heart can imagine."

*

"Words are also actions, and actions are a kind of
words."

ON FRIENDS

"A friend may well be reckoned the masterpiece of nature."

*

"It is one of the blessings of old friends that you can afford to be stupid with them."

*

"A man's growth is seen in the successive choirs of his friends."

*

"Friendship, like the immortality of the soul, is too good to be believed."

*

"The only way to have a friend is to be one."

DAVID GRAHAM

—

ALSO BY DAVID GRAHAM

Inside the Mind of George Bernard Shaw

The Very Best of Clint Eastwood

The Very Best of Roger Moore

The Very Best of Kirk Douglas

Made in the USA
Columbia, SC
05 January 2024

29924569R00037